T0071107

Lightwaves

Bob Chilcott

for SATB (with divisions) and piano

vocal score

MUSIC DEPARTMENT

OXFORD
UNIVERSITY PRESS

OXFORD
UNIVERSITY PRESS
Great Clarendon Street, Oxford OX2 6DP,
United Kingdom

Oxford University Press is a department of the University of Oxford.
It furthers the University's objective of excellence in research, scholarship,
and education by publishing worldwide. Oxford is a registered trade mark of
Oxford University Press in the UK and in certain other countries

© Oxford University Press 2021

Bob Chilcott has asserted his right under the Copyright, Designs
and Patents Act, 1988, to be identified as the Composer of this Work

First published 2021

Impression: 1

All rights reserved. No part of this publication may be reproduced,
stored in a retrieval system, or transmitted, in any form or by any means,
without the prior permission in writing of Oxford University Press

Permission to perform this work in public (except in the course of divine worship)
should normally be obtained from a local performing right licensing organization,
unless the owner or the occupier of the premises being used already holds
a licence from such an organization. Likewise, permission to make and
exploit a recording of these works should be obtained from a
local mechanical copyright licensing organization

Enquiries concerning reproduction outside the scope of the above
should be directed to the Music Rights Department, Oxford University Press,
at music.permissions.uk@oup.com or at the address above

ISBN 978-0-19-353530-5

Music and text origination by Katie Johnston
Printed in Great Britain on acid-free paper by
Halstan & Co. Ltd, Amersham, Bucks.

Contents

1. Telescope 4
2. Harbour 14
3. Bulb 20
4. Sundown 26
5. Leaf 32

Composer's note

Lightwaves was written for the youth choir festival in Eugene, Oregon, **picfest**, a festival with which I have had a long and happy association. Way back in 2016, the Festival Director, Peter Robb, and I discussed the idea of me writing a piece with the poet Charles Bennett on the theme of light. We saw the idea as a way of projecting light, in both a physical and metaphorical sense, as a positive force in our world. The texts touch on stars, the guiding light of a lighthouse, the electric light bulb, and the sun. The final song speaks of the light needed for trees to grow, a particularly emotive and pressing theme as I write this in autumn 2021.

The five songs have various voicings within the SATB format, so there is flexibility to perform them separately or as a set.

Lightwaves was composed as part of the new **picfest Commissions Project** for *Lift Every Voice 2020*, a festival in Eugene, Oregon. The event features youth choirs from across North America and around the world. Funding for **picfest's** innovative commissioning model pairs a Principal Patron with the Festival Chorus, whose members serve as both individual Singer Patrons and the ensemble premiering the work.

The choirs comprising the 2020 Festival Chorus were: Cantabella Children's Chorus (California); Children's Chorus of Maryland; Columbia Choirs (Washington); Emerald Valley Honor Choir (Oregon); Phoenix Boys Choir (Arizona); Pacific Youth Choir (Oregon); and The St. Louis Children's Choirs (Missouri).

Three months before the curtain was slated to rise on the festival, COVID-19 exploded onto the world stage, resulting in an historic shutdown of public gatherings and shuttering of performance venues. The premiere of *Lightwaves* was postponed until a return to choral events was possible.

At the time of publication, plans are underway for **picfest** to resume festival presentation with *Lift Every Voice 2022*. The premiere will add a second group of choirs as additional Singer Patrons. The names of both 2020 and 2022 Festival Chorus members and their choirs can be found at picfest.org/singer-patron/

Duration: *c.*15 minutes

Composed as part of the ***picfest Commissions Project*** *for* 'Lift Every Voice 2020'

Lightwaves

Charles Bennett (b. 1954)

BOB CHILCOTT

1. Telescope

Music © Oxford University Press 2021. Text © Charles Bennett. Reproduced by permission of the author.

Printed in Great Britain

OXFORD UNIVERSITY PRESS, MUSIC DEPARTMENT, GREAT CLARENDON STREET, OXFORD OX2 6DP

The Moral Rights of the Composer have been asserted. Photocopying this copyright material is ILLEGAL.

9
Near. Far. Then. Now.
13
Soon. Late. Dim. Bright.
17
Young. Old. Star - light.

22
mf
Here is light from a dis - tant star come to be where you are.
mf
mf
26
it's ar - rived at
How far it trav - elled, what it passed, does not mat - ter, it's ar - rived at
last.
30
f
last, ar - rived at last. Light from a star dis - tilled by time en - ters your eye,
f
f

34
ex - cites your mind. Light from a star dis - tilled by
37
en - ters your eye,
time en - ters your eye, your eye, ex - cites your
40
mf
mind.
mf
mf

UPPER VOICES (SEMI-CHORUS)
44
mp
Dis-tant. Close. Fast. Slow.
S.
A.
T.
B.
48
Near. Far. Then. Now.

52
Soon. Late. Dim. Bright.
Soon. Late. Dim. Bright.

56
Young. Old. Star - light.
Young. Old. Star - light.

60
mf
S.
A.
Im - ag-ine stars as thoughts that flash In the night as they pass.
T.
B.
mf
mf
from a star.
65
Bright for a mo - ment, here you are, filled with won - der from a star, from a
70
f
star. Light from a star dis - tilled by time en-ters your eye, ex - cites your
f
f

74
light from a star.
mind. Light from a star dis - tilled by time, light from a star, a
78
UPPER VOICES (SEMI-CHORUS)
Light from a star,
f
Light from a star,
light from a star,
S.
A.
star. Light from a star dis - tilled by time en-ters your eye, ex - cites your
T.
B.

82
light from a star,
light from a star, a star,
light from a star, a star,
en-ters your eye,
mind. Light from a star dis - tilled by time en-ters your eye, your
86
mf
ex-cites your mind.
mf
eye, ex-cites your mind.
mf
mf

90
mp
Dis-tant.
p
Dis-tant.
mp
Dis-tant.
p
Dis-tant.
mp
p
mp
p

rit.
94
pp
Dis-tant.
pp
Dis-tant.
pp
rit.
pp

2. Harbour

Still ♩ = c.60
SOPRANO
ALTO
p
I am the
TENOR
BASS
p
Still ♩ = c.60
p sonore
con Ped.

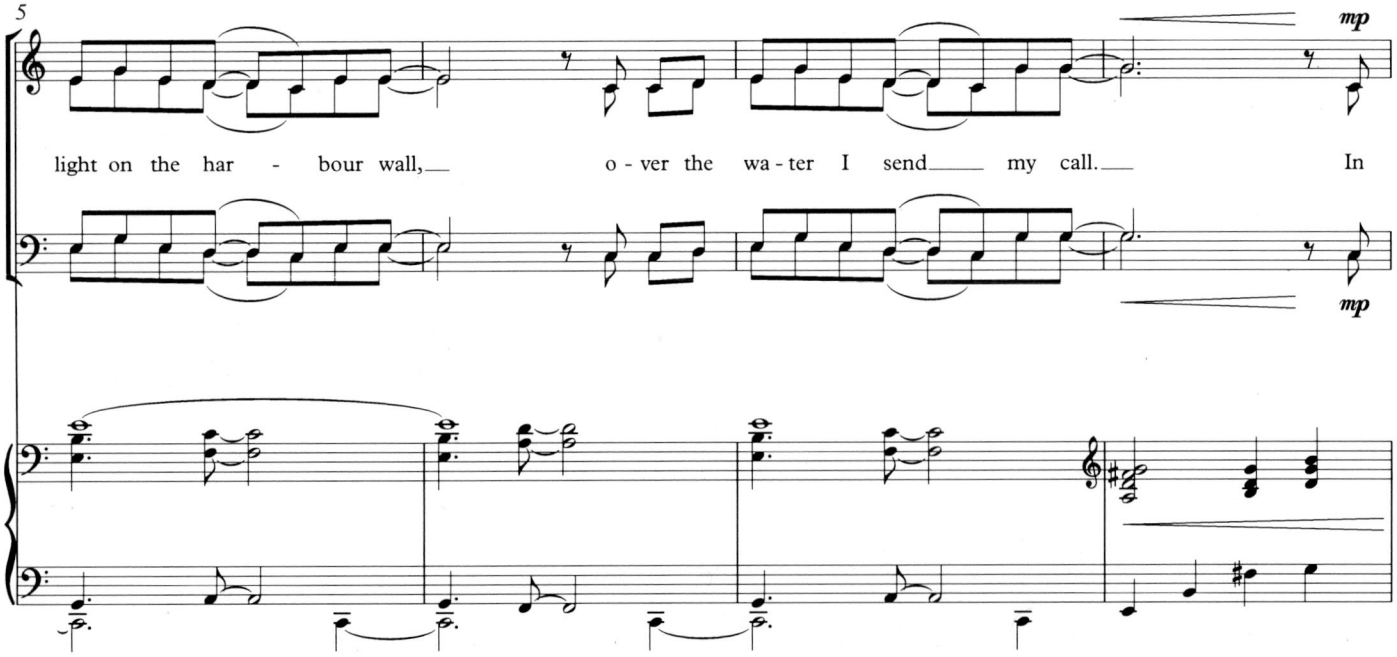
5
mp
light on the har - bour wall, o - ver the wa - ter I send my call. In
mp

storm,
9
mf
mp
tem - pest, hur - ri - cane, or storm, or storm, I am
mf
mp
mp
mf
mp
13
p
mp
calm, calm.
In the dark - est
mp
p
In the dark - est night you've known,
p
mp

years go by with - out a dawn.
mf
18
night you've known, years go by with - out a dawn.
But I am wait - ing,
years go by with-out a dawn.
mf
mf
bright and true,
f
22
I am wait - ing, bright and true,
here for you.
I am wait - ing, bright and true,
I am wait - ing, bright and true,
f
f

26
guide me through the deep - est night;
Port and star - board, left and right,
guide me through the deep - est, deep - est
guide me through the deep - est, deep - est
let me find the har - bour light,
mf
f
mp
30
night; let me find the har - bour light,
the har - bour
night; let me find the har - bour light,
mf
f
mp

34
p
light.
Time to leave those waves be - hind,
p
p sonore
UPPER VOICES (SEMI-CHORUS)
39
p
ah
ah
mp
Come from deep, dis-turb-ing
mp
S.
A.
dis - cov - er peace true voy - ag - ers find.
Come from deep, dis -
T.
B.
mp
mp

43
mf
ah
seas,
mf
p
-turb - ing seas, home to me,
mf
p
mf
p
47
rit.
p
ah
pp
oo
pp
home to me, to me.
pp
rit.
pp

3. Bulb

With energy ♩ = c.108
SOPRANO
ALTO
f
E - lec - tri - ci - ty, how I wish I
f
5
un - der - stood your shock - ing kiss.
Po - si - tive, ne - ga - tive,
9
black or red, cut the wire, be - side my bed.
con Ped.

14
p sost.
Small, tame sun
mp
p sost.
20
in my bed - side light, you wait all
26
day to help me read my book.
32
mp
mf
If my sis - ter cries, you show me to her
mp
mf

38
room. In the dark of morn - ing you
44
are my win - ter dawn.
f
50
f
E - lec - tri-ci-ty, how I wish I un - der - stood your shock - ing kiss.
55
Po - si - tive, ne - ga - tive, black or red, cut the wire, be - side my

59
p
bed.
You fell si - lent
mp
p
65
once
when the lines went down.
71
mp
You are the i - dea I have when all my thoughts are
mp
77
mf
o - ver.
Com - f'ta - ble to - geth - er,
mf

83
mp
like a hap - py cou - ple. At the end of the
mp
89
p dolce
poco rit.
day you watch me sleep.
p dolce
a tempo
96
f
E - lec - tri - ci - ty, how I wish I
f
100
un - der - stood your shock - ing kiss.
Po - si - tive, ne - ga - tive,

104
ff
black or red, cut the wire, the wire. E - lec - tri - ci - ty,
ff
108
how I wish I un - der - stood your shock - ing, shock - ing kiss.
112
Po - si - tive, ne - ga - tive, black or red, cut the wire, be - side my bed,
117
fff
be - side my bed, be - side my bed.
fff

4. Sundown

Flowing ♩ = c.72
TENOR
BASS
mf
con Ped.
5
mf
Sky - swim-mer!
High - ris-er!
Eye-in-the-sky!
Sweet - sur-pris-er!
9
f
Bob-by be - daz - zler!
Hy-dro-gen storm!
Play - time's o - ver:
time to come
f

13
mf
mp
down, come down. In my wa - ters,
mf
mp
18
mf
dark and deep, float your fie - ry globe and sleep. Bring me all the aer - ial news,
mf
23
ah
f
snooze a - while in cool - ing blues. Sky - swim-mer!
f
27
High - ris - er! Eye - in - the - sky! Sweet - sur-pris-er! Bob-by be - daz - zler!

31
Hy-dro-gen storm! Play - time's o - ver: time to come down,
35
mf
come down.
mp
Feel the wa - ter,
mf
mp
39
smooth as silk, like Cle - o - pat - ra, sink in milk.
mf
I will heal your
mf
43
wounds and bless skin that craves a sweet ca - ress.

47
p
Sky - swim-mer!
High - ris - er!
Eye - in - the - sky!
p
50
mp
mf
Sweet - sur - pris - er!
Bob - by be - daz - zler!
Hy - dro - gen storm!
mp
mf
53
f
mf
Play - time's o - ver:
time to come down,
come
f
57
mp
down.
Be - drag - gle gold - en fea - thers now
mf
mp

61
in my bri - ny un - der - tow.
Come on in, the wa - ter's cool,
65
plunge in - to my swim - ming pool.
Sky - swim - mer!
f
f
69
High - ris - er!
Eye - in - the - sky!
Sweet - sur - pris - er!
72
Bob-by be - daz - zler!
Hy-dro-gen storm!
Play - time's o - ver, o - ver.

ah
ff
76
Sky - swim-mer!
High - ris - er!
Eye - in - the - sky!
Sweet - sur-pris-er!
ff
f
80
Bob - by be - daz - zler!
Hy - dro - gen storm!
Play - time's o - ver:
f
83
time to come down,
come down,
mf
mf
rit.
88
mp
down,
come down,
come down.
p
mp
p

5. Leaf

* The *8va* instruction only applies to the uppermost note of the chord.

8
mp
O - pen in spring.
Drop like a tear.
mp
mp
12
p
mp
My days are short.
They come and go.
I feed on light,
p
mp
p
mp
16
p
so a tree may grow.
p
8va
p

20
T.
B.
TENORS & BASSES unis.
p
Some-times I wish our skin could
23
un - der-stand the light the way a tree does, the way a tree does.
26
S./A. unis.
p
S.
A.
The light would be our food, all na - tions on Earth would be a for - est, be a

29
S.
A.
mp
mf
for - est. Per - haps we'd be wis - er at last, dis -
T.
B.
mp
mf
Per - haps we'd be wis - er, wis - er at
mp
32
is
mp
-cov-'ring all we need, dis - cov-'ring all we need is rain and sun, is
mp
last, dis - cov-'ring all we need is rain and sun, is
mf

35
rain and sun.
We'd
(b)
rain and sun.
mp
38
mf
breathe the Earth clean as we turned il - lu - mi -
mf
mf
41
-na - tion in - to en - light - en - ment, en - light - en - ment,

44
p
en - light - en - ment.
p
p
47
mp
slow - ly grow - ing old - er by
Each year we'd love our leaves,
mp
mp
49
poco rit.
let - ting them go, let - ting them go.
let - ting, by let - ting them go, go.
let - ting them go, go, go.
poco rit.

a tempo
52
8va
p
56
p
mp
I am a leaf.
I last a year.
O - pen in
p
mp
8va
mp
60
p
spring.
Drop like a tear.
My days are short.
p
p

64
mp
They come and go. I feed on light, so a
mp
mp
tree may grow,
68
mf
tree may grow, may grow, I feed on light,
mf
mf

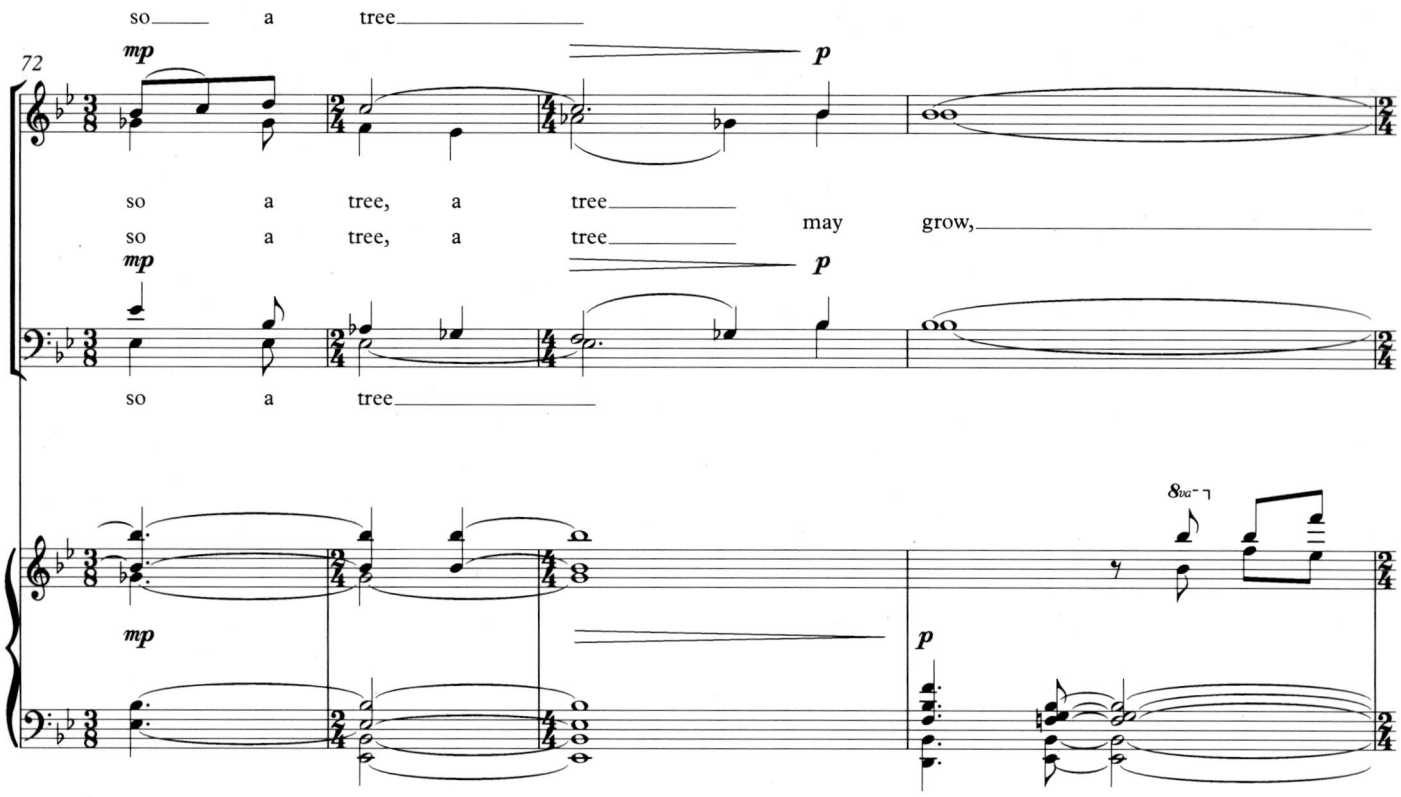
so a tree
72
mp
p
so a tree, a tree
so a tree, a tree
may grow,
mp
p
so a tree
8va
mp
p

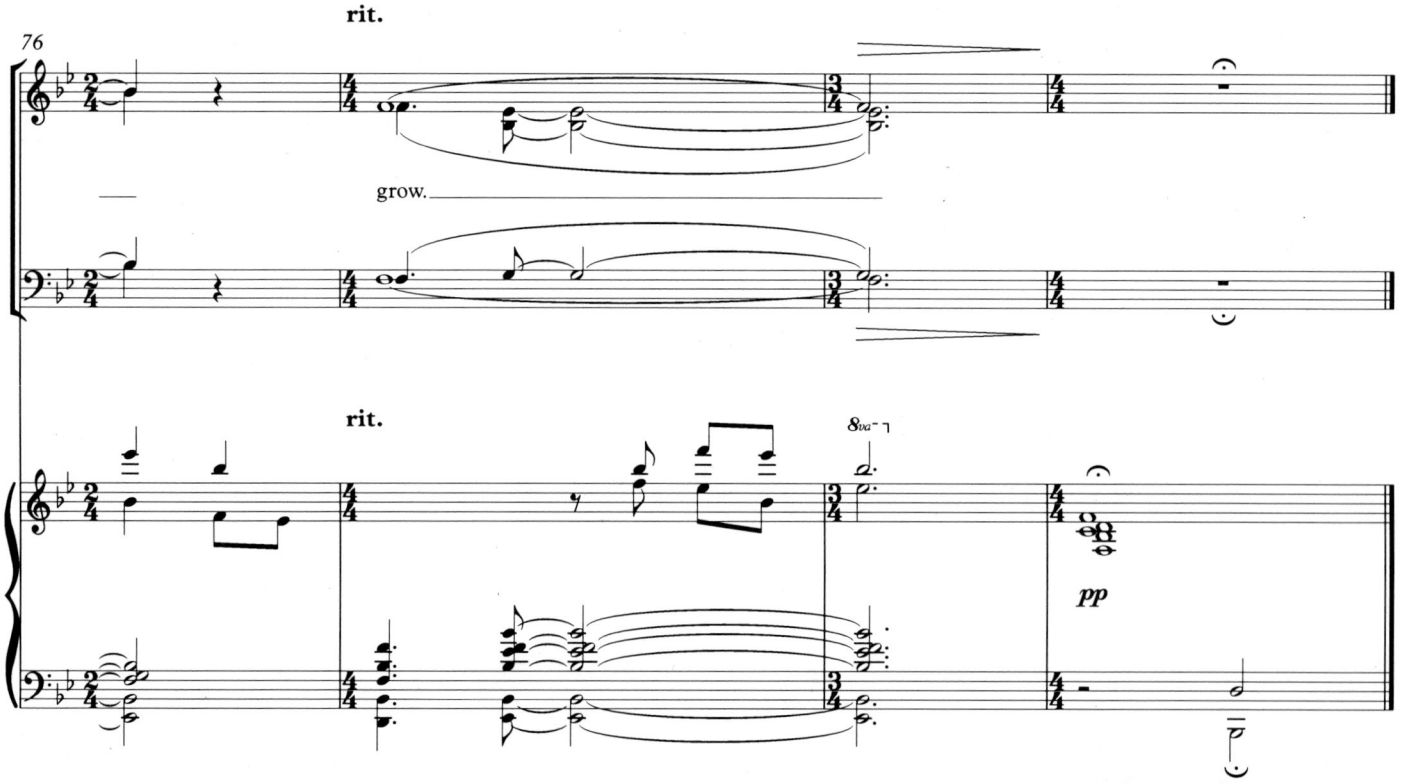
rit.
76
grow.
rit.
8va
pp